FOOD & HOW TO COOK IT!

EGGS AND DAIRY

BY JILLIAN POWELL

WITH RECIPES BY CLARE O'SHEA

WAYLAND

First published in 2009 by Wayland
Copyright © Wayland 2009

Wayland
338 Euston Road
London NW1 3BH

Wayland Australia
Level 17/207 Kent Street
Sydney NSW 2000

Commissioning editor: Jennifer Sanderson
Designer: www.rawshock.co.uk
Photographer: Andy Crawford
Illustrator: Ian Thompson
Hand model: Camilla Lloyd
Proofreader and indexer: Susie Brooks
Consultant: Clare O'Shea - Clare has taught food
technology for more than 17 years in various
London-based schools. She is currently Head of
Food Technology at London Academy, where she
teaches years 7 to 13. The Academy delivers GCSE
Hospitality and Catering to years 10 and 11, A Level
Food Technology and the Food Hygiene Certificate.

British Library Cataloguing in Publication Data
O'Shea, Clare.
    Eggs & dairy. -- (Food and how to
cook it)
    1. Dairy products--Juvenile literature.
    2. Eggs--Juvenile literature.
    3. Cookery (Dairy products)--Juvenile
literature.
    4. Cookery (Eggs)--Juvenile literature.
    I. Title II. Series III. Powell, Jillian.
    641.3'7-dc22

ISBN: 978 0 7502 5662 9

Printed in China

Wayland is a division of Hachette Children's Books,
an Hachette UK company.
www.hachette.co.uk

Picture Acknowledgements:
All photography by Andy Crawford, except: Agripicture Images/
Alamy: 34; ArkReligion.com/Alamy: 35; iStockphoto.com: 9, 16,
21T, 27, 28, 29T, 36, 37, 42, 43 ;Jaubert Bernard/Alamy: 40; Joerg
Boethling/Still Pictures: 17; Nigel Cattlin/Alamy: 18; Ellen Denuto/
Getty Images: 4; Enigma/Alamy: 19; Gallo Images/Getty Images:
20; Juniors Bildarchiv/Alamy: COVER, 6; Taylor S. Kennedy/
Getty Images: 24; Stockbyte/Getty Images: 8T; 3D4Medical.com/
Getty Images: 11

Note:
In preparation of this book, all due care has been exercised with regard
to the advice, activities and techniques depicted. The publishers regret
that they can accept no liability for any loss or injury sustained. Always
follow manufacturers' advice when using kitchen appliances and kitchen
equipment.

The website addresses (URLs) included in this book were valid at the
time of going to press. However, because of the nature of the Internet, it is
possible that some addresses may have changed, or sites may have changed
or closed down since publication. While the authors and publishers regret
any inconvenience this may cause the readers, no responsibility for any such
changes can be accepted by either the authors or the publishers.

Contents

Eggs, dairy foods and a balanced diet

Eggs and dairy products are found in an enormous range of foods – as ingredients, you may not even know you are eating them! Dairy foods include milk, cream, butter, yoghurt and cheese, which can be eaten as they are or cooked into delicious dishes.

Where do eggs and dairy foods come from?

Eggs and dairy foods are the products of animals, usually reared on farms. Most of the eggs we eat come from hens, while cows are the main source of milk. These animals may be farmed intensively indoors or 'free range' outdoors. Some farms are organic, creating their produce without the use of chemicals such as routine drugs or pesticides on crops. Eggs and dairy foods may be bought from local suppliers, or imported from abroad.

Choosing what we eat

The foods people eat, or their diet, vary around the world, partly depending on the climate and what grows best in particular areas. Personal beliefs and culture also affect our food choices. Many people object to eating meat or fish and instead follow a vegetarian diet. For them, eggs and dairy foods can be an important source of protein. Vegans however, do not eat dairy foods or eggs as they come from animals. Their diet is based entirely on plant foods.

A healthy diet

Our diet is an important part of a healthy lifestyle. There are five main food groups that contain different nutrients that work together to keep the body healthy. These groups are often shown on a 'food plate', where you can see the proportions in which they should be eaten (see page 5).

Added to these food groups is water. We need about six to eight glasses of water each day to keep our bodies healthy.

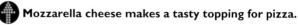
Mozzarella cheese makes a tasty topping for pizza.

The food plate

Fruit and vegetables: Full of vitamins and minerals, these foods protect our body and reduce the risk of heart disease, stroke and some cancers. The fibre in them helps to bulk up our food and keep our digestive system healthy. Fruit and vegetables are low in fat, so they fill us up without unnecessary calories.

Carbohydrates: These provide us with energy. Starchy carbohydrates, which include grains and cereals, should make up about 30 per cent of the food we eat. Starchy carbohydrates are an important source of energy for sportsmen and women because they release the energy slowly, keeping the body going for longer.

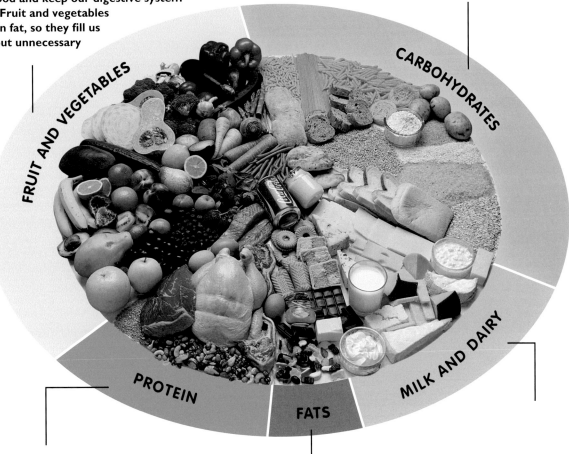

Protein: This builds and repairs our bones, muscles, skin, hair and tissues. Meat, fish, eggs and pulses, which provide body-building proteins, should make up about 15 per cent of our total daily diet.

Fats: These keep us warm and can also be stored in the body for energy. Foods that are high in saturated fats (fats from animal sources) or sugar, such as cakes, biscuits and crisps, should be eaten only in small amounts (about 8 per cent of our total diet). Fats found in oily fish, olives and nuts and seeds are called unsaturated fats. Saturated fats are linked to an increased risk of heart disease. Eating unsaturated fats is a healthier alternative.

Dairy: Dairy products include milk, butter, yoghurt and cheese. They are packed with nutrients, such as calcium, magnesium, Vitamin K, zinc and protein, and help to build strong bones and teeth. Yoghurt is full of good bacteria and improves our immune system and digestive health. It is best to eat cheese in moderation because it can be high in saturated fat.

FOOD FACTS

Teenage boys need 1,000 milligrams (mg) of calcium a day and girls need 800mg a day. A glass of milk (150ml) provides 234mg of calcium, while 40g Cheddar cheese provides 288mg.

Looking at eggs

Eggs are an important and versatile part of our diet. Cooked on their own they are a naturally healthy food – and they can also be used to make a variety of less healthy treats.

Where do eggs come from?

Birds, fish, and animals such as turtles and crocodiles, lay eggs to produce their young. Eggs that are fertilised by a male can grow and hatch into babies. We eat eggs that have not been fertilised – mainly hens' eggs, but also duck, goose and quails' eggs. Fish eggs, such as salmon and cod roe and caviar (sturgeon eggs), are also edible and are served as a delicacy in some parts of the world.

Which eggs to buy?

You might notice a variety of hen eggs on the supermarket shelves. Eggs come in different sizes and colours, depending on the type of chicken that laid them. They may also be free range or factory farmed. Many people object to the conditions in factory farms, where hens are kept in cages instead of being allowed to roam free. This also affects the eggs' flavour, as these chickens are raised on a controlled diet.

Why eat eggs?

Eggs contain a high amount of protein and many important vitamins and minerals. Proteins, which we need to grow and repair our bodies, are made from amino acids. The body can make some amino acids but it must take others (which are called essential amino acids) from our food. The protein in eggs contains all the essential amino acids that we need for a healthy body. Eggs are also rich in Vitamin A, which is important for healthy eyes, skin and bones, Vitamin B12, which is needed for the blood and nervous system, and Vitamin D, needed for strong bones and teeth. The minerals in eggs include iodine, phosphorus, calcium and iron – all of which are essential for a healthy body.

 Scratching about in soil or straw is natural behaviour for chickens.

 Eggs are traditionally sold by the dozen (12) or half dozen (6).

FOOD FACTS

Eggs are such a good source of protein that other protein-rich foods are measured against them. One egg provides about as much protein as 25 grams of lean meat, fish or poultry.

Food	Protein rating
Eggs (whole)	100
Eggs (whites)	88
Poultry	79
Fish	70
Lean beef	69
Cows' milk	60
Peanuts	55
Soy beans	47
Peanuts	43

Cholesterol

One egg contains about 5 grams of fat (most of which is 'healthy' unsaturated fat) and 213 milligrams of cholesterol, mainly in the yolk. Cholesterol is a fatty substance that the body makes naturally and also takes from some foods. Our bodies need some cholesterol, and there are 'good' and 'bad' types but doctors recommend that we have no more than 300 milligrams a day from our diet as high blood cholesterol can lead to heart disease.

Dishes and customs

Eggs are a very versatile cooking ingredient and are used in many favourite dishes around the world, from French toast and Spanish omelette to the African dishes of chakchouka (eggs with peppers) and eggs on fried okra. Eggs also play an important part in many food customs that celebrate birth and new life. Easter eggs (painted or chocolate eggs) are a symbol of the resurrection of Christ in the Christian calendar. Muslims in the Middle East give wrapped eggs to newly-wed couples to bring good luck and health. In China, painted eggs are given as gifts when a baby is one month old, to celebrate the new life.

Cooking eggs

Eggs can be boiled in the shell, poached, fried, scrambled or baked. They can also be put to many different uses in cooking. Eggs can be whisked up and heated to thicken quiches, custards and flans, used to bind ingredients together, or painted on pastries to create a glossy glaze.

Timing it right

As eggs are heated, the proteins in them change. In raw eggs, the proteins form long chains of amino acids curled into a ball. When they are heated, the chains unfold and begin to bind together into a mesh and the egg starts to set, or coagulate. If eggs are cooked for too long or on too high a heat, too many bonds form and the texture becomes rubbery. In general, eggs should be cooked over a gentle heat and removed as soon as they are set.

Boiled eggs

Eggs for boiling should be taken out of the fridge and at room temperature before cooking. If they come straight out of the fridge, the shells can crack as the water heats. The water should be simmering rather than boiling before you place the egg in it. Soft-boiled eggs will take 3–5 minutes, and hard-boiled eggs 7–10 minutes.

Poached eggs

Eggs can be poached, out of their shells, in simmering water or in buttered poaching trays standing in a pan. If you are not using poaching trays, stir the simmering water to create a whirlpool effect, add the egg to the water and leave for the required time. A runny egg will take 2 minutes, but if you want a firm egg, this will take 4 minutes.

Boiled eggs are a protein-rich breakfast food.

Poached eggs and spinach are ingredients for the Italian dish eggs Florentine.

 Fried eggs are part of a traditional English breakfast, and are usually served with bacon.

Fried eggs

Fried eggs are cracked into hot fat or oil in a frying pan. The eggs should be allowed to settle and begin to go firm before gently lifting the sides and spreading the oil around. The heat can be turned up for a crispy white.

Scrambled eggs and omelettes

For scrambled eggs and omelettes, eggs must be beaten or whisked before cooking. Scrambled eggs are stirred into a frying pan of hot, melted butter until they just begin to coagulate. Continual stirring breaks them into creamy lumps.

 KNOW YOUR FOOD

Cool hard-boiled eggs under cold running water to stop the white turning grey.

For omelettes, butter or oil is heated in a frying pan before the beaten eggs are poured in and allowed to cook until almost set. Some cooks add a little milk or water to the eggs before they are added to the pan. You could also add ingredients such as mushrooms and grated cheese to add flavour to the omelette.

Baked eggs

A simple but tasty way of cooking eggs is to bake them in a hot oven. The egg should be carefully broken into a buttered dish or ramekin, then seasoned and dotted with butter. The dish is then placed in a roasting tin containing enough hot water to come halfway up its sides. Cooking takes about 15–20 minutes at 190°C/gas mark 5.

Binding and blending

Egg yolks contain emulsifiers – binding agents that help to blend and stabilise other ingredients. This makes eggs useful for thickening sauces and custards and also for binding together ingredients in fishcakes, meatloaves and burgers.

Raw eggs can be used to blend oil and vinegar or lemon juice to make a creamy mayonnaise. If the ingredients are shaken together to make a simple dressing, they will mix temporarily but separate again because oil is more dense than vinegar. However, when eggs are added, some of the amino acids in the egg stick to the oil and others to the vinegar, holding them together in a smooth blend.

Adding volume

When egg whites are whisked or beaten, they form a foam of air bubbles. Air becomes trapped between the chains of proteins as they unfold and mesh together. When the mixture is heated, the air bubbles expand and protein in the egg white coagulates around them. This traps the bubbles to give a light and airy texture. Egg whites can be used to puff up soufflés, and make fluffy omelettes, meringues and mousses. Whole eggs are beaten into cake mixtures to help produce a springy sponge.

Always use clean utensils when beating egg whites. Avoid using plastic bowls, as traces of grease or oil can spoil fluffy egg white. Once the egg whites have formed soft peaks, use them immediately or they will start to lose air and volume. They should be carefully folded into heavier ingredients, never the other way round.

Glazing

Eggs can be beaten and brushed onto bread or pastry before baking. As the egg proteins bake, they form a crispy golden glaze that not only looks attractive, but will also hold toppings such as nuts, seeds or breadcrumbs in place. Foods for frying, such as fishcakes and chicken breasts can be coated with an egg glaze and then dipped in breadcrumbs.

Storing and handling eggs

Eggs need careful handling and storage. They should always be kept in a refrigerator and used when they are as fresh as possible. Make sure you check the use-by date and avoid using eggs that are dirty or cracked. Once eggs have been cracked open, they should be used immediately. Egg whites can be stored in a sealed container in a fridge for a few days or frozen for later use.

FOOD FACTS

A beaten egg white can foam up to eight times its original size.

Fresh eggs

To test how fresh an egg is, put it in a glass of water. A fresh egg will sink; a less fresh egg will stand on its end and a stale egg will float. This is because as eggs get older, they lose moisture through the shell and take in more air, which makes the air pocket inside bigger and the egg lighter.

Food safety

It is important to follow food safety rules when using eggs. This is because some raw or lightly cooked eggs may contain harmful bacteria, such as salmonella, which can cause food poisoning. Very young children, pregnant women and sick

 These eggs are fresh, so they have sunk to the bottom of the bowl. Older eggs will stand on end, or if they are stale they will float.

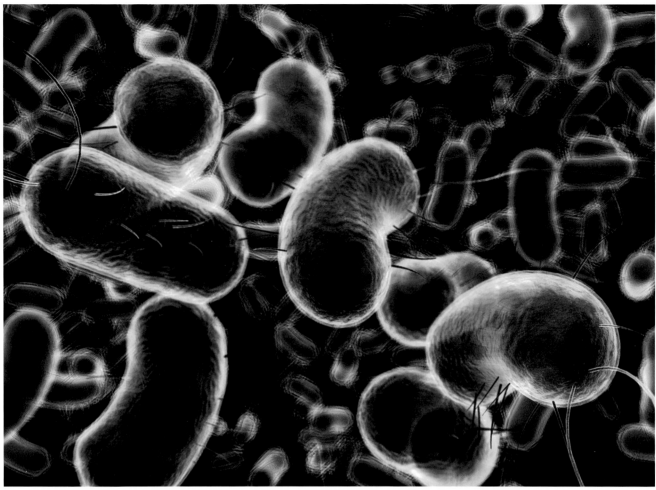

✚ **This is what salmonella bacteria look like when viewed under a microscope.**

or elderly people can be more at risk from these bacteria, so they should eat only eggs that are cooked right through and avoid eggs with runny yolks. For recipes using raw eggs, such as mayonnaise or ice cream, it is best to use pasteurised eggs. These come frozen or in liquid or powder form. They have been heat treated to kill harmful bacteria.

Technique		Description
	Breaking an egg	Break eggs into a separate bowl before adding to a recipe to avoid getting bits of shell in with other ingredients. Crack the egg in its middle against a bowl. Put your fingers into the centre of the crack and pull the two halves apart.
	Separating eggs	Crack the egg over a bowl. Keep the yolk in one half of the shell and then gently tip it into the other half of the shell so that the white falls into the bowl.

Meringues

A perfect summer's dessert, meringues are delicious served with any fruit, fresh cream and/or ice cream.

Ingredients
2 egg whites
50g caster sugar
fresh fruit, to serve
double cream, to serve

1. Preheat the oven to 140°C/ gas mark 1.

2. Whisk the egg whites until they just start to go stiff.

3. Gradually add the sugar, whisking all the time.

4. When all the sugar is added, the whites should be stiff and form peaks. They should be stiff enough to turn the bowl upside down without them moving.

5. Place baking parchment on a baking tray. Put the egg whites in a piping bag or use a spoon to make small pyramid shapes of egg whites.

6. Bake the meringues for approximately 1 hour until they are fully dry. When they are cool, they should come off the parchment very easily.

7. Whip the cream before serving it with the meringues and fresh fruit.

Bacon and mushroom quiche

SERVES: 2 | **PREPARATION TIME: 30 MINUTES** | **COOKING TIME: 50 MINUTES**

This quiche can be eaten hot or cold. It makes a delicious weekend brunch dish and is perfect for a summer picnic.

Ingredients
50g bacon
3 mushrooms, sliced
125ml milk
2 eggs
50g Cheddar cheese, grated
1 large tomato, sliced, plus extra
 for serving
sprig of parsley, to serve

For the pastry
100g plain flour
50g butter
pinch salt
30ml water

1. Preheat the oven to 190°C/gas mark 5. Grease an 18-cm flan dish.

2. Cut the rind off the bacon and cut the bacon into small pieces. Fry it over a medium heat until there is no pink left on it.

3. Add the mushrooms to the pan. Fry them until soft. Set aside the mushrooms and bacon to use later.

4. To make the pastry, rub the butter into the flour and salt with your fingertips until it resembles breadcrumbs (see page 47).

5. Stir in the water with a metal spoon to make a soft dough. If the mixture does not stick together, add a little more water.

6. Roll out the pastry to the same size as the flan dish, then line the dish with the pastry.

7. Put the milk in a jug and crack the eggs into it. Beat well to mix.

8. Put the bacon, grated cheese and mushrooms into the flan dish and pour over the milk and egg mixture.

9. Place the tomato slices over the top of the quiche.

10. Bake for 30–40 minutes until golden brown and firm to touch.

11. Garnish with the parsley and serve hot or cold with slices of fresh tomato.

Butter cup scrambles

These eggy baskets are perfect for a brunch meal or a weekend breakfast. You can add slices of cherry tomato, too for extra flavour.

Ingredients
125g butter
8 slices thin bread
5 eggs
1 tablespoon fresh parsley, chopped
90ml milk
100g garlic sausage
2 sticks of celery, chopped
2 spring onions, trimmed and finely chopped
50g Cheddar cheese, grated

1. Preheat the oven to 200°C/ gas mark 6.

2. Melt 100g of the butter and allow it to cool, but not to set.

3. Trim the crusts from the bread and dip each slice in the melted butter to coat evenly.

4. To make the butter cups, use the buttered bread to line 8 deep Yorkshire pudding trays, leaving the corners of each slice of bread uppermost.

5. Bake the cups for 15–20 minutes, until golden.

6. In the meantime, break the eggs into a bowl, then add the parsley and milk and beat with a fork.

7. Cut the sausage into slices. Melt the remaining butter in a pan, add the sausage and fry until cooked.

8. Add the egg mixture to the pan with the sausages and cook over a low heat until it begins to set.

8. Stir in the celery, spring onions and cheese and mix well.

9. When the cups are ready, divide the egg mixture evenly between each cup and serve immediately.

Classic omelette

SERVES: 1	PREPARATION TIME: 15 MINUTES	COOKING TIME: 7–10 MINUTES

This classic omelette recipe makes a quick and easy meal.

Ingredients
2 eggs
1 tablespoon water
salt and pepper
1 tablespoon vegetable oil
fried mushrooms, to serve

1. Lightly beat the eggs, water, salt and pepper together in a bowl.

2. Heat the oil in a frying pan over a medium heat. Turn up the heat to high.

3. Pour the eggs into the frying pan, tilting the pan as you do this.

4. Allow the uncooked egg to run to the edges, while the centre cooks.

5. While the centre is still runny, fold over the omelette and place it on a serving plate. Serve with some fried mushrooms

COOK'S TIP

To make a cheese omelette, add 50g grated Cheddar cheese after pouring in the eggs.

French toast

SERVES: 2	PREPARATION TIME: 20 MINUTES	COOKING TIME: 10 MINUTES

French toast is delicious with fruit, but it can also be served with bacon and grilled tomatoes.

Ingredients
2 eggs
½ teaspoon sugar
½ teaspoon salt
100ml milk
4–6 slices white
     bread
1 tablespoon butter
syrup, to serve
fruit, to serve
icing sugar, to serve

1. Break the eggs into a bowl and beat gently.

2. Stir in the sugar, salt and milk.

3. Place the bread, one slice at a time, into the egg mixture. Turn the bread over so that each slice is covered in egg on both sides.

4. Melt the butter in a frying pan or griddle over a medium heat.

5. Place the eggy bread on the griddle and cook until brown underneath. Turn over and cook the other side.

6. Serve with the syrup and fruit and a dusting of icing sugar.

Looking at dairy foods

Dairy foods include milk and foods made from milk, such as butter, cream, cheese, ice cream, fromage frais and yoghurt. They add great flavour and variety to our diet – and in the right amounts, they are good for us, too.

Where do dairy products come from?

Most of the milk we use is produced by cows, but people also use milk from goats, sheep, buffaloes, yaks and other animals. These animals may be kept on commercial farms with dairies, or in some places a family may own one or two animals to supply just the milk they need. In dairies and factories, milk is processed in different ways to turn it into a wide range of dairy foods.

Why eat dairy foods?

Milk and dairy foods are an excellent source of protein, potassium, phosphorus and Vitamins A and D. They are also the richest dietary source of calcium. Calcium is needed to build strong bones and teeth and reduce the risk of diseases, such as osteoporosis, and tooth decay. Some studies show that increasing our intake of calcium, potassium and phosphorus can lower blood

 Dairy products come in a variety of forms, textures and flavours.

pressure and so help to keep the heart healthy. Milk is important for babies and children as it helps them to grow and develop healthy bodies with strong muscles, bones and teeth. It is also a useful food for the elderly and people recovering from illness, as it is easy to digest.

Milk fat

Milk and dairy foods contain fat, which we need to keep us warm and give us energy. However, too much saturated fat can make the blood sticky and clog the arteries, leading to heart disease. Milk can be skimmed or semi-skimmed to reduce the fat content. Half-fat and low-fat milk and dairy foods are healthy options as they contain little saturated fat. They have the same amount of protein and calcium as whole or full-fat milk, and most vitamins except Vitamins A and D, which are lost during skimming. Extra milk solids and vitamins are often added to improve the flavour and increase the nutrients in low-fat dairy products. Sometimes, extra sugar is added, too, which is not good for us if eaten in large quantities.

This water buffalo is being milked by hand in Mumbai. Water buffalo are the chief dairy animals in India.

FOOD FACTS

We need Vitamin D to help our bodies absorb calcium. Vitamin D is made by the body when the skin is exposed to sunlight. It is also found in dairy products, egg yolks and fish.

Milk

On its own, milk is one of the most 'complete' foods as it is packed with important nutrients. What is more, you do not need to cook it – it tastes good just as it is!

Types of milk

There are many different types of milk. Most of the milk we use has been pasteurised, which means it has been treated to kill any harmful bacteria or enzymes that might be present in raw milk. Some milk is homogenised – processed to break up the globules of milk fat so the cream does not separate out and the milk stays smooth and uniform.

Milk that is heat-treated (UHT) has a longer shelf life than fresh milk. Milk can also be evaporated or condensed by boiling off the water content to leave concentrated milk solids. Condensed milk may have sugar added to it to sweeten and preserve it. Dried or powdered milk can also be stored for long periods, and mixed with water or added to dry ingredients for cooking.

KNOW YOUR FOOD

Evaporated milk can be whipped and used as a low-fat alternative to cream.

 In 1856, the French scientist Louis Pasteur discovered that heating liquids to high temperatures kills bacteria. This process is called pasteurisation, and it protects the purity and flavour of milk. Milk is pasteurised in hygienic plants such as this one.

 In many countries, the different colours on milk packaging refer to the fat content of the milk. For example, in the United States, skimmed milk bottles have green labels, while milk with 1 per cent fat has blue labels.

Organic milk and milk products come from cows that have grazed on pasture that is free from chemical fertilisers or pesticides.

Why drink milk?

Milk contains more than ten important nutrients, including protein, carbohydrate, Vitamin A (for healthy growth, skin and eyes), B vitamins (which help us to take energy from food and keep the blood and nervous system healthy), Vitamin D (for healthy bones) and important minerals including calcium, potassium and phosphorus. Milk is the richest dietary source of calcium. A pint of milk a day provides all the calcium we need.

Milk also contains milk sugars, or carbohydrates, called lactose. Some people can be lactose-intolerant, which means that their bodies are unable to digest milk sugars. This is because they have a shortage of the enzyme lactase, made by cells in the small intestine. This enzyme is needed to break down milk sugars so they can be absorbed into the blood. People who are lactose-intolerant can choose alternatives to dairy products, such as soya or rice milk and spreads and drinks made from these.

Different milks

Goat and sheep's milk are more easily digested than cow's milk and can often be drunk by those who are lactose intolerant. They are popular in Mediterranean countries, such as Greece, where there is less pasture for grazing cattle. About 15 per cent of the world's milk production is from water buffaloes, which are farmed in South-east Asia, South America and Italy. This milk is higher in protein and calcium and contains less cholesterol than cow's milk. Dried or powdered milk is used in places where the climate makes the storage and transportation of fresh milk difficult.

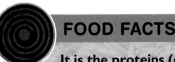

FOOD FACTS

It is the proteins (called casein) in milk that reflect light and make milk look white.

Using milk

Milk can be drunk hot or cold or mixed into drinks such as smoothies, shakes, tea, coffee and hot chocolate. As a cooking ingredient, milk adds body and makes dishes smooth and creamy.

Milk in cooking

Milk can be used to make custards, pancakes, waffles and milky rice or bread puddings. In South America, the popular sweet dulce de leche is made by gently heating milk and sugar to form a rich caramel. You can find something similar in a banoffee pie. Milk can also be used as an ingredient in many savoury dishes, including soups, white sauces and risottos. It may be used to poach fish, or to soak breadcrumbs for meatloaves or burgers.

Storing milk

Milk should be kept refrigerated and used within three or four days. It should always be kept covered as it can pick up flavours from other foods in a fridge, and away from sunlight, which can destroy the vitamin content. Some milk can be frozen, but this can break down the casein proteins and make the milk look 'curdled'.

Heating milk

Milk should be used at room temperature for cooking. It should always be heated slowly and gently to avoid burning. This is because when milk is heated, some proteins separate out and settle at the bottom of the pan where they can easily scald. Milk proteins can also cluster on the surface of the milk, forming a skin as water in the milk evaporates. To prevent a skin forming, cover the saucepan with a lid.

 Milk tarts can be flavoured with nutmeg or cinnamon like this South African version.

Curdling

When milk is added to soup or other hot dishes it can curdle. This happens when the casein proteins begin to coagulate and clump together. Too much heat, acid (such as vinegar or lemon juice) and salt can all cause curdling. To avoid it, use a full-fat milk for cooking. The higher fat content makes milk more stable. Remember to heat it through gently and add any salt just before serving.

 Iced coffee, made with chilled milk, is increasingly popular in the summer when it is too warm to drink hot coffee.

Classic white sauce

MAKES: 300ML	PREPARATION TIME: 1 MINUTE	COOKING TIME: 15 MINUTES

White sauces are used as a basis for cheese sauces and other sauces such as béchamel sauce.

Ingredients
25g butter
25g plain white flour
300ml milk

1. Melt the butter in a saucepan.

2. Blend in the flour and cook over a low heat, stirring all the time with a wooden spoon. The mixture will become a thick lump, which is called a roux.

3. Add a little milk and beat vigorously until the mixture leaves the sides of the pan. Add a little more milk and beat again. Allow the milk to boil and thicken, then add more milk. Continue to do this until all the milk has been used.

4. When all the milk has been added, bring the sauce to the boil and allow to simmer for 5 minutes.

COOK'S TIP

You can add cheese, parsley or chopped garlic – or a combination of all three – to add flavour to the sauce.

Pancakes

Traditionally pancakes are eaten on Shrove Tuesday, the day before the Christian period of Lent starts – but these are so tempting, you will want to eat them all year round!

Ingredients
1 egg
250ml milk
100g plain flour
1 tablespoon caster sugar
2 tablespoons vegetable oil
juice 1 lemon

1. Break the egg into a jug and add the milk. Mix well.

2. Put the flour in a bowl, add the milk mixture and whisk to make a smooth batter. Pour the batter back into the jug.

3. Heat a little of the oil in a small frying pan over a medium heat.

4. When the oil is hot, pour in just enough batter to cover the bottom of the pan.

5. Cook the pancake until the bottom is golden brown. Turn the pancake over and cook the other side.

6. When the pancake is cooked, put it on a plate, sprinkle with lemon juice and sugar and roll it up.

7. Return the pan to the heat, add a little oil and when it is hot, add more batter and cook the next pancake in the same way. Continue to do this until all the batter has been used.

COOK'S TIP

Make a hot chocolate sauce and pour this over the pancakes instead of lemon and sugar.

Bread and butter pudding

SERVES: 3–4 | **PREPARATION TIME: 20 MINUTES** | **COOKING TIME: 40 MINUTES**

This winter pudding can be served with custard or cream – but it is so delicious that you may just want to eat it as it is!

Ingredients
25g butter
3 slices bread, without crusts
50g dried fruit
1 tablespoon sugar
350ml milk
2 eggs, beaten
pinch nutmeg
single cream,
  to serve

1. Preheat the oven to 180°C/ gas mark 4.

2. Grease an ovenproof dish with a little of the butter. Use the rest to spread onto the bread. Cut the bread into triangles.

3. Put a layer of bread into the dish and sprinkle with some of the fruit and sugar. Continue with these layers until all the bread, fruit and sugar has been used – you should end with a layer of bread.

4. Warm the milk in a saucepan, but do not let it boil. Add the milk to the eggs and mix well.

5. Pour the milk and egg mixture over the bread. Sprinkle the pudding with nutmeg and set it aside for 10 minutes.

6. Bake in the oven for 30–40 minutes, until golden brown and set. Serve with cream.

Rice pudding

SERVES: 3–4 | **PREPARATION TIME: 10 MINUTES** | **COOKING TIME: 2 HOURS**

This hearty pudding is an old favourite. It is everything a pudding should be – sweet, filling and mouth-wateringly good!

Ingredients
50g pudding rice
50g sugar
500ml milk
15g butter, diced

1. Preheat the oven to 150°C/ gas mark 2.

2. Wash the rice in a sieve under cold running water. Put it in an ovenproof dish and sprinkle it with the sugar.

3. Pour over the milk and dot with the butter.

4. Bake for about 2 hours until the rice is soft.

COOK'S TIP

Add sultanas and raisins for a sweeter pudding.

Cheese

There are thousands of different types of cheese. They reflect a world of different flavours and cooking styles, although they all start off in the same way – as milk.

Making cheese

Cheese can be produced by hand in small dairies or by machines in giant factories. It is made by separating the solid curds from the runny whey in milk. Pasteurised milk is pumped into large vats and warmed, then treated with a bacterial culture. This ferments and flavours the milk and helps it to coagulate or become solid. Animal or vegetable rennet is then added, and enzymes in the rennet separate the thick curds from the runny whey proteins.

To make soft cheeses, such as cottage cheese and cream cheese, the whey is drained off as the curds coagulate. These cheeses are ready to eat within hours or days. To make firm cheeses, the curds are stirred or stirred and heated to remove the whey, then salted and pressed into moulds and stored to mature. This can be for several months, depending on the type of cheese. Salt improves the flavour and texture of the cheese and also acts as a preservative.

 These Swiss cheeses are being carefully stored so that they can ripen or mature.

Unpasteurised cheeses

Some cheeses are made with unpasteurised milk. These include Stilton, Brie and Camembert cheese. While such cheeses are prized for their flavour, there is a small risk that they might grow harmful bacteria, including listeria. Blue cheeses and soft cheeses that are ripened in the mould, such as Brie or Camembert, should be avoided during pregnancy because listeria could harm the unborn baby.

This range of cheese includes **English Cheddar (1), Swiss Emmental (2), Italian Parmesan (3), Dutch Edam (4), French Brie (5)** and **Greek feta (6).**

Cheese from other animals

Cheese can also be made from the milk, pasteurised or unpasteurised, of other animals. Goat's cheese is made by warming the milk then separating out the curds and whey using rennet. The curds are drained and pressed into round cheeses, which can be stored in cloth and eaten as a soft cheese after a few days or allowed to mature and form a rind in brine. Greek feta is traditionally made from sheep's milk. The milk is curdled with rennet, then the curds are drained and cut into slices (or 'feta' in Greek). These are salted and stored for anything from a week to several months in the salty whey or brine. Mozzarella is an Italian cheese traditionally made with water buffalo milk. When the curds have been separated from the whey they are 'spun' by dipping them into hot water so they form long strings. These are kneaded and folded together to make a stretchy elastic ball of cheese that is plunged into cold water then stored in brine or oil.

Feta cheese (1) is made from sheep's milk, while mozzarella (2) is made from buffalo milk and goat's cheese (3) from the milk of goats.

FOOD FACTS

It takes 10 litres of milk to make 1 kilogram of cheese.

Texture and flavour

The texture, flavour and nutritional content of a cheese vary according to how it is made, the type of milk it is made from, and differences in the starter culture. Swiss cheeses, such as Gouda and Edam, are made using a culture that produces gas, forming holes in the cheese. Blue cheeses, such as Stilton and Danish blue, have a blue type of mould added. The cheeses are stored, then pierced to make air holes that allow the mould to spread through the cheese. Some cheeses have herbs, fruit or nuts mixed in to add flavour and texture.

Curds, whey or cream can all be used to make different types of cheese. Mascarpone is an Italian cream cheese that is made from cream fermented by lactic acid. It can be used in pasta sauces, risottos and desserts. Ricotta (which means re-cooked) is made from scalded whey. It is like a grainy, thick sour cream. Quark, or curd cheese, is a fresh cheese that is traditionally made from curd without using rennet, but with lactic acid as the starter culture. It is similar to South Asian paneer, and Mexcian queso blanco.

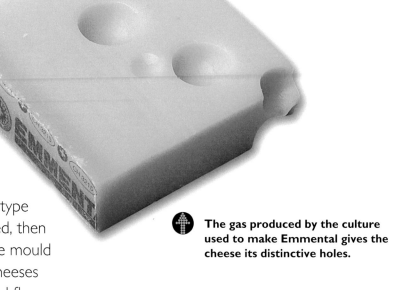

 The gas produced by the culture used to make Emmental gives the cheese its distinctive holes.

Cheese rind

Fresh cheeses have no rind. Soft, ripened cheeses, such as Brie and Camembert, and some goat's cheeses have a soft and supple rind. Some rinds form naturally on the cheese as it matures, as with Stilton. Others are 'washed rinds' that form when the cheese is washed in beer, brine or another liquid. Washing helps friendly bacteria to grow, ripening and flavouring the cheese. Cheese can also have edible coatings of nuts, herbs or peppercorns. Some have inedible rinds of wax, twigs or cloth.

Camembert has a soft rind. The cheese becomes runny at room temperature.

Why eat cheese?

As cheese is a concentrated form of milk, it is a nutritious food and a rich source of protein and calcium in the diet. Some cheeses are high in saturated fats, so they should be eaten in moderation. Full-fat cheeses include firm cheeses, such as Cheddar and Parmesan, and some soft cheeses, including mascarpone, which can have nearly 50 per cent fat content. Cheeses made from skimmed milk have a reduced fat content, but they may be less tasty as the milk fat gives cheese its flavour. Brie is a medium-fat cheese, while low-fat cheeses include cottage cheese, fromage frais and quark.

Storing cheese

Cheese should be kept in a refrigerator and removed a short while before serving. Wrap firm cheeses to stop them from drying out and picking up flavours from other foods. Parchment paper or aluminium foil is better than plastic wrap or cling film because it allows the cheese to 'breathe' without drying out. This is important because the living enzymes and bacteria in cheese need air and moisture to survive. Strong-smelling cheeses, such as Gorgonzola and blue cheeses, should be wrapped and stored in an airtight container so they do not pass on their flavour to other foods.

Serving cheese

Fresh cheeses, such as cottage cheese, ricotta and mascarpone, should be kept chilled and used straight from the fridge. Some semi-soft cheeses, including feta and mozzarella, are best stored in a container filled with water or brine to keep them moist. Serve firm cheeses at room temperature to get the full flavour. Ripened cheeses, including Camembert and Brie, should be taken out of the fridge a few hours before use.

 Slice or grate hard cheeses, such as Cheddar, just before you are ready to use them, to avoid them drying out.

FOOD FACTS

Cheese can be a useful source of protein, calcium and Vitamin B12 in vegetarian diets, but vegans and some vegetarians will not eat cheese made with animal rennet, which is extracted from the stomach of calves.

Cooking with cheese

Cheese is a tasty and versatile ingredient that can be eaten in snacks and sandwiches as well a range of cooked dishes. Popular examples include macaroni cheese, cauliflower cheese, pizza toppings and creamy desserts like cheesecake.

Cooking methods

Different types of cheese cook in different ways. This depends largely on the cheese's texture, which may vary from soft and creamy to crumbly or hard and dense. Some firm cheeses, such as Greek halloumi, are suitable for grilling or frying; others break down easily and can be used in baking or sauces. The Swiss cheese Emmental melts smoothly over a low heat and makes a delicious fondue (hot cheese dip). Greek feta can be crumbled over salads or into salad dressings.

Hard cheeses, including Cheddar and Parmesan, cook best and melt easily when they are grated, sliced or shredded.

KNOW YOUR FOOD

Cheese should always be cooked over a gentle heat, as too high a temperature can make it tough and rubbery.

 Grating cheese makes it easy to spread as a topping. Mozzarella cheese is grated and sprinkled over pizza bases.

Cheese dishes

Grated hard cheese can be baked with onions and other ingredients in cheese pies and tarts, or melted into sauces for dishes such as macaroni cheese, pasta bakes and cauliflower cheese. It can also be mixed with eggs and milk to make cheese soufflés, quiches and flans, or added to pastry or dough to make cheese straws, scones or bread. Under the grill, it makes a crispy 'gratin' topping for potato or vegetable dishes. Soft cheeses, such as ricotta, cream cheese and mascarpone, can be whipped into rich desserts including mousses, cheesecakes and the Italian tiramisu. Some cheeses are used in salads. For example, mozzarella is traditionally added to tomatoes and avocado pears to make tricolore, an Italian salad. Feta cheese is teamed with tomatoes, olives, onions and cucumber to make a Greek salad.

 Cheese is used to make a fondue. Vegetables or bread are dipped into the cheese before eating.

Welsh rarebit

SERVES: 4	PREPARATION TIME: 20 MINUTES	COOKING TIME: 15–20 MINUTES

The success of this dish – sometimes mistakenly called Welsh rabbit – lies in cooking it over a low heat until all the cheese has melted.

Ingredients
200g Cheddar cheese, grated
25g unsalted butter
1 teaspoon English mustard
3 tablespoons milk
salt and pepper
4 slices toast
griddled tomatoes, to serve

1. Put the cheese, butter, mustard and milk in a saucepan over a low heat.

2. Stir the mixture until it is smooth and creamy and coats the back of a wooden spoon. Season to taste.

3. Spoon the cheese onto the toast, then grill until it is golden.

4. Remove from under the grill and cut each slice of toast in half. Serve immediately with the tomatoes.

Cheese scones

These scones can be eaten on their own or sliced and spread with butter. They are delicious served as an accompaniment to soup.

Ingredients
100g medium oatmeal
150ml milk
butter, for greasing
150g plain white flour, plus extra
     for dusting
½ teaspoon baking powder
½ teaspoon salt
25g Edam cheese, grated

1. Put the oatmeal in a large bowl, pour over the milk and leave to soak for 30 minutes.

2. Preheat the oven to 180°C/gas mark 4. Lightly grease a baking tray.

3. Sieve the flour, baking powder and salt into the oatmeal mixture. Add the cheese and mix well to make a soft dough.

4. Turn the dough onto a lightly floured surface and knead for 2 minutes (see page 47), until soft and elastic.

5. Roll out the dough to 2cm thick, then use a pastry cutter to cut out 6 scones.

6. Place the scones on the baking tray and bake for 20 minutes. Serve warm or cold.

COOK'S TIP

Add crushed garlic and/or chives for extra flavour.

Macaroni cheese

SERVES: 2 **PREPARATION TIME: 20 MINUTES** **COOKING TIME: 40 MINUTES**

This baked pasta dish is an old favourite. You can add bacon and spring onions for extra flavour.

Ingredients
100g short-cut macaroni
100g cheese
25g flour
500ml milk
salad, to serve

1. Fill a large saucepan of water and place over a medium heat to boil. When the water is boiling, add the macaroni and cook according to the packet instructions.

2. In the meantime, preheat the oven to 180°C/gas mark 4.

3. To make the cheese sauce, put the cheese, flour and milk into a saucepan on a low heat. Stir the sauce continuously in a figure of eight movement and gradually increase the heat. The sauce should thicken to coat the back of a wooden spoon.

4. When the pasta is cooked, drain it before adding it to the cheese sauce. Stir to mix well.

5. Place the macaroni in an ovenproof dish and bake for 20 minutes until it is golden brown. Serve with a side salad.

Cheese-filled pancakes

MAKES: 4 **PREPARATION TIME: 20 MINUTES** **COOKING TIME: 10–15 MINUTES**

The spinach in these pancakes is packed with iron, while the cheese is calcium rich and low in fat.

Ingredients
100g wholemeal flour
1 egg
25ml milk
2 tablespoons vegetable oil

For the filling
450g spinach
225g cottage cheese
salt and pepper

1. Put the flour, egg and milk into a mixing bowl and mix well to make a smooth batter.

2. Heat a little of the oil in a frying pan. Pour a ladleful of batter into the middle of the pan and spread it until it covers the bottom of the pan.

3. Cook the pancake for 2 minutes and then turn it over and cook the other side. When cooked, place the pancake on a plate. Cook all the pancakes in the same way.

4. Cook the spinach in a frying pan over a low heat for 2–3 minutes. Remove the spinach from the heat, drain off any excess water, then add the cottage cheese. Season to taste and mix well.

5. Return the spinach mixture to the heat for 3 minutes.

6. Place spoonfuls of the mixture on each pancake. One at a time, roll up the pancakes and serve.

Savoury party treats

MAKES: 30 | **PREPARATION TIME: 40 MINUTES** | **COOKING TIME: 20–30 MINUTES**

These party snacks look as good as they taste and are sure to impress.

Ingredients
butter, for greasing
500g ready-made puff pastry
milk, for brushing
1 bunch fresh chives
50g dried cranberries
250g cream cheese

1. Preheat the oven to 180°C/gas mark 4. Grease 2 large baking sheets.

2. Roll out the pastry to about 1cm thick and cut out circles of about 2cm in diameter.

3. Place the circles on the baking trays and brush with a little milk.

4. Bake for 10–15 minutes until slightly brown. Remove from the oven and place on a wire rack to cool.

5. In the meantime, finely chop the chives and cut the cranberries in half.

6. Mix the cream cheese with the chives and place teaspoons of the mixture on each pastry base.

7. Top with the dried cranberries and serve.

Strawberry cheesecake

SERVES: 6 | **PREPARATION TIME: 40 MINUTES** | **CHILLING TIME: 3 HOURS**

This cheesecake does not need baking, making it quick and easy to make.

Ingredients
200g digestive biscuits
100g butter
140ml double cream
1 teaspoon icing sugar
250g cream cheese
140ml strawberry yoghurt
100g fresh strawberries,
    stalks removed

1. To make the base, put the biscuits into a plastic bag and, using a rolling pin, crush them until they resemble fine breadcrumbs.

2. Melt the butter in a saucepan over a medium heat. Remove from the heat and add the biscuit crumbs. Stir well.

3. Spread the biscuits mixture over the base of a 20cm cake tin.

4. To make the filling, whisk the double cream and icing sugar together until they make a mousse-like mixture.

5. Fold the cream cheese into the cream. Fold the yoghurt into the cream mixture.

6. Pour the filling over the base and leave in a fridge to set for about 1 hour.

7. Remove the cake from the fridge and decorate with the strawberries. Return the cake to the fridge and leave to set for a further 2 hours.

8. Remove from the fridge and serve.

Mozzarella cheese pizza

SERVES: 2 | **PREPARATION TIME: 40 MINUTES** | **COOKING TIME: 20–30 MINUTES**

You cannot go wrong with this mozzarella pizza – it is easy to make and delicious to eat.

Ingredients
200g strong white bread flour,
    plus extra for sprinkling
7g dried yeast
1 teaspoon salt
125ml warm water
1 tablespoon vegetable oil,
    plus extra for greasing

For the topping
2 tomatoes
1 garlic clove, peeled and
    finely chopped
3 sprigs fresh basil
250g mozzarella cheese

1. Preheat the oven to 200°C/ gas mark 6.

2. Place the flour, yeast and salt in a large mixing bowl. Make a well in the middle (see page 47).

3. Place the water in a jug and add the oil. Pour the liquid into the well and mix to make a soft dough.

4. Turn the dough out onto a lightly floured surface and knead for 10 minutes (see page 47).

5. Roll out the dough into a round shape and place on a greased baking tray. Cover with cling film and leave in a warm place to rise for 20 minutes.

6. In the meantime, slice the tomatoes and grate the cheese. Tear the basil into small pieces.

7. When the base is ready, bake it in the oven for 5 minutes. Remove from the oven and add the tomato, cheese, garlic and basil.

8. Bake the pizza for 20 minutes until golden brown. Serve immediately.

COOK'S TIP

Add some salami or pepperoni slices for a meatier pizza.

Butter and cream

Butter is made using the cream from cow, sheep or buffalo milk. It is a useful form of fat for cooking, adding a rich flavour to all manner of sweet and savoury dishes.

Making butter

To make butter, the cream is skimmed from the milk and pasteurised to destroy any harmful enzymes or bacteria. The cream is then churned until the fat globules separate out from the runny buttermilk and begin to stick together as grains or granules of butter. Next, the butter is drained and mixed with water until a smooth texture is achieved. Some butter has salt added to it. It can also have air or nitrogen gas whipped through it to make it spreadable at cold temperatures.

The good and bad in butter

Butter contains protein, calcium, phosphorus and Vitamins A, D and E. Full-fat butter is about 80–82 per cent milk fat, 16–17 per cent water and 1–2 per cent milk solids. Salted butter contains about 3 per cent salt, and slightly salted butter around 1 per cent. Butter is high in saturated fats, so it should be eaten in moderation. For low-fat diets, butter is available with a reduced fat content. However, 'light' or reduced fat butters are not suitable for frying or baking because they contain more water and are less stable when heated.

FOOD FACTS

It takes 20 litres of whole milk to produce 1 kilogram of butter. Salt adds flavour and gives the butter a longer shelf life.

 In this dairy, butter is being shaped by hand using a traditional butter pat.

Cooking with butter

Butter can be used for spreading, frying, sautéing and grilling. It is also used to grease pans or dishes to prevent cakes and bread sticking and as a glaze for pies. Butter can be flavoured with garlic, mustard or herbs to use with fish or meat dishes. In baking, it adds a melt-in-the-mouth quality to pastry, cakes, biscuits and pies. Butter can also be added to hollandaise, beurre blanc (a light, buttery sauce) and other sauces to give a glossy, smooth texture and a rich taste.

Clarified butter

To make clarified butter, butter is heated to boiling point so that the water content evaporates and the milk solids settle. This leaves a pure, clear liquid fat. In India, the clarified butter, called ghee, is made from buffalo milk. It is widely used in Indian cooking for dishes such as dhal and curries and to make traditional sweets. In some Hindu ceremonies, statues of gods are washed in ghee and it is also thrown into altar fires or used to light holy lamps during festivals.

 This woman is cooking with ghee for a festival in honour of a Hindu spiritual leader, Guru Tegh.

Buttermilk

Buttermilk can be produced by fermenting the runny whey left behind after churning butter. It can also be made by adding a bacterial culture to skimmed milk. Buttermilk has a slightly sour, acidic taste and is a useful ingredient when baking soda bread and scones.

KNOW YOUR FOOD

To stop butter burning, cook it over a low heat and combine with a little oil or sprinkle a few grains of salt in the pan before heating.

Cream

To produce cream, milk is heated and spun until the globules of fat separate out. These are skimmed off, then cooled and pasteurised, sterilised, or heat-treated to make long-life UHT cream. Cream is graded by the amount of butterfat it contains. Thick clotted cream can contain up to 55 per cent butterfat. Double cream contains 48 per cent or more, and whipping cream 35 per cent or more. Single cream contains at least 18 per cent butterfat, and half cream at least 12 per cent. The higher the percentage of butterfat, the more fattening the cream!

Soured cream

Cream can have a bacterial culture added to make sour cream or crème fraiche – a thick cream with a sharp flavour. Soured cream is a useful ingredient in soups, stews, cakes and cheesecakes and makes a tasty topping for fruit, desserts or baked potatoes. It can also be used as a marinade before cooking, as its slight acidity tenderises meat and will hold seasonings in place.

Type of cream	
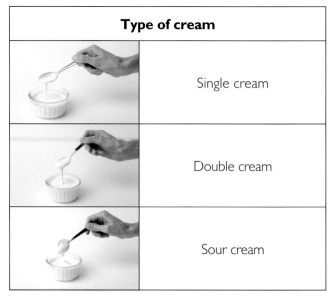	Single cream
	Double cream
	Sour cream

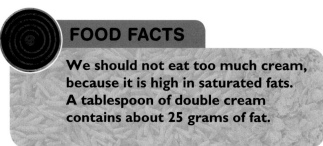

FOOD FACTS

We should not eat too much cream, because it is high in saturated fats. A tablespoon of double cream contains about 25 grams of fat.

Sour cream and chives make a tasty topping for baked potatoes.

 Scones with jam and cream are part of a traditional cream tea served in the south-west of England.

Cooking with cream

Cream can be used to make a huge range of sweet dishes, including the Italian dessert panna cotta, crème caramel, fruit fools and mousses. It is also used to make creamy sauces for meat or pasta and stews such as goulash. Thicker creams with a higher fat content, such as double cream and crème fraiche, are best for thickening sauces as they are more stable and less likely to curdle or separate when heated. Cream can be 'scalded' (heated almost to boiling point) to make crème brûlée and ice cream. Whipping cream can be whisked into sauces to add richness, or folded into cakes or mousses for a light texture. It is also delicious served alone with fruits, as in the traditional English strawberries and cream.

 COOK'S TIP

It is easier to whisk whipping cream when the cream and bowl are cold, because the fat globules hold together. Stop whisking as soon as the cream stands up in soft peaks.

Storing cream

Cream should be stored in the fridge and used within a few days once opened. Like milk, cream should be kept covered to stop it picking up flavours from other foods.

Chocolate chip cookies

MAKES: 6 | PREPARATION TIME: 40 MINUTES | COOKING TIME: 20-30 MINUTES

These cookies are perfect for dunking in a cup of tea or a glass of ice-cold milk.

Ingredients
125g plain white flour, plus extra for
    sprinkling
100g butter
25g caster sugar
1 tablespoon beaten egg
½ teaspoon baking powder
100g milk chocolate
    chips

1. Preheat the oven to 180°C/gas mark 4. Line a baking tray with greaseproof paper and sprinkle over some flour.

2. Cream the sugar and butter to make a smooth, creamy mixture (see page 47).

3. Add the egg and mix well.

4. Sieve the flour and baking powder over the butter mixture. Add the chocolate chips and stir well.

5. Make 6 ball shapes out of the dough and place on the baking tray. Press down on the balls to flatten them into a cookie shape.

6. Bake for 20 minutes. Remove from the oven but leave on the baking tray for 5 minutes before allowing to cool on wire rack.

Chocolate truffles

MAKES: 30 | PREPARATION TIME: 20–30 MINUTES | COOKING AND CHILLING TIME: 2 HOURS

Truffles are incredibly more-ish, and these are no exception!

Ingredients
140ml double cream
300g milk chocolate
50g unsalted butter
4 shortbread biscuits, roughly
    crumbled
85g mixed dried fruit
zest of 1 orange
cocoa powder, for rolling

1. Put the cream into a small saucepan and bring to the boil. Remove from the heat.

2. Put the chocolate and butter into a bowl and place over a saucepan of boiling water until melted.

3. Add the cream, biscuits, dried fruit and orange zest to the chocolate. Stir well. Place in the fridge for 1 hour.

4. Use a teaspoon to scoop out the truffle mixture and form it into small balls.

5. Roll each ball in the cocoa powder before placing it in a paper case. Leave in the fridge to set.

COOK'S TIP

Try dipping the truffles in melted white chocolate instead of rolling them in cocoa powder.

Crème brûlée

SERVES: 6 **PREPARATION TIME: 20 MINUTES** **COOKING AND CHILLING TIME: 7 HOURS 30 MINUTES**

This traditional French dessert is popular around the world. The individual pots make it perfect for a more formal dinner.

Ingredients
750ml single cream
6 egg yolks
1 level teaspoon caster sugar
1 tablespoon vanilla essence
2 teaspoons Demerara sugar

1. Put the cream in a bowl over a pan of simmering water (see page 47).

2. In another bowl, beat the egg yolks with the caster sugar and vanilla essence.

3. When the cream is warm, stir in the egg mixture and cook until the cream has thickened enough to coat the back of a wooden spoon.

4. Pour the mixture into small dishes or ramekins and leave to chill for 4 hours.

5. Sprinkle the Demerara sugar over the top of the puddings.

6. Put the crème brûlées on a tray of ice cubes and place under a hot grill until the sugar melts.

7. Put the puddings back in the fridge and chill for a further 3 hours before serving.

COOK'S TIP

Forest fruits, such as strawberries and raspberries can be served with this dessert.

Yoghurt

Yogurt is made from milk that has been pasteurised and fermented by adding a bacterial culture. We can buy yoghurt ready-to-eat in many flavours, but it is also a healthy and versatile cooking ingredient.

Making yoghurt

Yoghurt can be made from whole, skimmed or dried milk – from cows, goats, sheep or even buffaloes. When bacteria are added to milk, they produce lactic acid, which turns the lactose or milk sugars into lactic acid. Lactic acid breaks down proteins in the milk, making it coagulate and thicken. This process also gives yoghurt its tangy, sharp or slightly sour taste.

Differences in the type of milk, the starter culture and the way the yoghurt is fermented produce many different varieties including set, stirred, frozen and drinking yoghurt. Some yoghurt is heat-treated to prolong its shelf life, but this kills many of the friendly bacteria found in live or bio yoghurts.

Yoghurt for health

Yoghurt is a good source of protein, calcium and Vitamins B6 and B12. All yoghurts contain the harmless bacteria lactobacillus bulgaricus and streptococcus thermophilus. Live yoghurts have added 'friendly' bacteria that can boost the body's immune system, keep the digestive system healthy and fight stomach bugs.

Fat content

Yoghurt varies in fat content. Thick, creamy yoghurts made from whole milk, sometimes with cream added, have 3–4 per cent fat. Some Greek-style or set yoghurts are especially thick and creamy and can contain 10 per cent fat. They should be eaten in moderation. Low-fat yoghurts have up to 2 per cent fat, and very low fat yoghurts have less than 0.5 per cent fat.

 Yoghurt is sold in individual pots for convenience. Some pots, such as this one, are made from glass so that they can be recycled.

Set yoghurt: These yoghurts ferment in the pots and set into a firm, jelly-like texture. Some are flavoured, others are natural but have a fruit layer in the bottom of the pot.

Bio yoghurt: These yoghurts have 'friendly' bacteria, such as lactobacillus acidophilus and bacillus bifidus, added to them. They usually have a milder, less acidic taste than non-bio varieties. They can be flavoured with fruit, such as strawberries.

SET YOGHURT

BIO YOGHURT

FLAVOURED YOGHURT

NATURAL YOGHURT

Flavoured yoghurt: These yoghurts have been flavoured with whole fruit, fruit purée or syrup or other flavourings, such as chocolate, toffee or nuts. Although low-fat varieties of flavoured yoghurts are available, they are often higher in sugar than natural yoghurt.

Natural yoghurt: These yoghurts have had no flavours added and they can be sharp or mild, runny, creamy or firm and set. The smoothest and creamiest varieties are often higher in fat and calories.

FOOD FACTS

Some people who are lactose-intolerant can eat yoghurt, because the active cultures produce the enzyme lactase, which helps the body to break down and digest milk sugars.

Cooking with yoghurt

Yoghurt can be used as a low-fat replacement for many other dairy products in cooking. It works well in soups, sauces, curries and stews, as well as creamy puddings.

Yoghurt dishes

Natural yoghurt can be used as a topping for desserts, cereals and baked potatoes or mixed with herbs or spices to make dips or side dishes. In Indian cooking, a raita made with yoghurt, herbs and cucumber is often served alongside curried dishes as it cools the flavours of chillies and other hot spices. In Greece, the popular dish tzatziki is made from yoghurt mixed with cucumber, garlic, oil and vinegar. The slight acidity of yoghurt also makes it a useful marinade that tenderises meat. It can be added to pasta sauces, stews or curries, too, and used in baking cakes, scones and soda bread.

Yoghurt as an ingredient

Yoghurt is an excellent substitute for double cream, sour cream or crème fraiche as it has a similar smooth taste and texture. It can also be used to replace milk, butter or oil in baking. As an ingredient, it can make baked goods fluffy and moist, and reduce calories and fat content. It may also be combined with baking soda to help scones and cakes rise. Some recipes use yoghurt as a low-fat alternative to cream cheese. Mixing yoghurt with lemon juice or vinegar makes a light, refreshing salad dressing.

 The cool, tangy taste of natural yoghurt compliments hot, spicy curries.

 Natural yoghurt served with chopped fresh fruit makes a healthy, low-fat dessert that is bursting with vitamins and minerals.

Handling and heating

Yoghurt should always be handled and heated gently, because over-mixing or cooking at too high a temperature can make it curdle or separate and can also destroy friendly bacteria. To stop yoghurt separating, add it at the end of cooking time to soups and sauces, and fold it in gently until just heated through. Yoghurt can also be mixed with a little cornflour or plain flour before adding it to a hot dish, as this will help to prevent curdling.

Storing yoghurt

Yoghurt should be stored in a refrigerator and used by the use-by date or within a few days of opening. Some yoghurts can be frozen in their pots for about two months. They should be completely thawed before eating.

 KNOW YOUR FOOD

Do not use aluminium or copper pans for cooking yoghurt as the acidic content can react with the metal.

 **FOOD FACTS**

As natural yoghurt gets older, it becomes sharper in taste. This is because it can go on fermenting, increasing acidity.

Banana frozen yoghurt

This frozen yoghurt is lower in fat than ice cream, but it tastes just as good!

Ingredients
3 ripe bananas
450g low-fat natural yoghurt
2 nectarines, to serve

I. Peel and mash the bananas in a large bowl.

2. Gradually add the yoghurt and beat well to make a smooth, creamy mixture.

3. Pour the mixture into a freeze-proof container with a lid. Cover and freeze for 30 minutes.

4. Tip the mixture back into the bowl and whisk for 2 minutes.

5. Return the mixture back to the freeze-proof container, cover and freeze for another hour.

6. Remove from the freezer and whisk again before returning to the freezer until set. Each time you whisk it, the mixture should be smoother and creamier.

7. When ready to serve, halve the nectarine, remove the stone and slice each half in half again.

8. Place nectarine pieces around scoops of the frozen yoghurt to serve.

COOK'S TIP

Swap the banana for ripe mango or use a combination of the two.

Cucumber raita

SERVES: 4 | **PREPARATION TIME: 20 MINUTES** | **COOKING TIME: NO COOKING**

Raita is perfect for cooling down a hot curry or for dipping poppadoms.

Ingredients
250ml natural yoghurt
½ cucumber
2 sprigs fresh coriander, plus extra for garnishing
1 teaspoon black pepper
pinch chilli powder

1. Pour the yoghurt into a bowl and beat it.

2. Grate the cucumber and finely chop the coriander.

3. Add the cucumber, coriander, pepper and chilli powder to the yoghurt and mix well. Pour into a bowl to serve.

COOK'S TIP

Try using a chopped, roasted aubergines instead of cucumber.

Blueberry muffins

MAKES: 12 MUFFINS | **PREPARATION TIME: 20 MINUTES** | **COOKING TIME: 20 MINUTES**

Blueberry muffins are always popular as a brunch-time treat. They are best eaten on the day they are made.

Ingredients
100g butter
300g plain flour
½ teaspoon baking powder
½ teaspoon salt
2 eggs
75g caster sugar
25ml natural yoghurt
100g blueberries

1. Preheat the oven to 180°C/gas mark 4. Place 12 paper cases in a muffin tray.

2. Melt the butter in a pan, then remove it from the heat.

3. In the meantime, sieve together the flour, baking powder and salt in a large mixing bowl.

4. Beat the eggs, then add them with the sugar and yoghurt to the butter. Mix well.

5. Add the butter mixture to the sifted flour and stir well to make a smooth batter.

6. Add the blueberries and mix well.

7. Place spoonfuls of the batter in the paper cases and bake for 20 minutes until slightly brown.

8. Remove from the oven and serve.

# Glossary

amino acids	parts of food that make up proteins and help to break them down when food is being digested
bacteria	tiny living organisms; some are helpful in the body; others can be harmful
bacterial culture	harmless bacteria, used to start fermentation
béchamel	a white sauce made with butter, flour and milk
buttermilk	the liquid left after churning butter
carbohydrate	a nutrient that gives the body energy
cholesterol	a substance made by the body and found in some foods; some types of cholesterol are good for us; others can be harmful
coagulate	to thicken into a semi-solid or solid mass
curd	the solid part of milk, mainly casein proteins
digestive system	parts of the body that work together to process food
emulsifier	a substance that breaks down fat so that it can dissolve in water
enzyme	a chemical agent that changes food into substances that our bodies can absorb
ferment	to bring about change so that sugars turn into carbon dioxide and alcohol
fibre	the bulky part of food, known as roughage, that is needed for digestion
glaze	to give a glossy coating
goulash	a type of meat and vegetable stew
immune system	the body's natural defences, which fight off infections and diseases
lactic acid	a chemical compound found in sour milk
lactose	milk sugars

milk solids	the solid part left when water has been evaporated from milk
mineral	a substance, such as iron, that is found in the soil and the foods we eat
nutrient	any part of a food that gives the body energy or the goodness it needs to grow and stay healthy
osteoporosis	a bone disease in which the bones become brittle and more likely to break
pasteurised	treated by pasteurisation to kill harmful bacteria
preservative	a chemical substance that is added to food to make it last longer
protein	a nutrient that helps the body to grow and repair itself
pulses	the seeds of pod-bearing plants, such as beans, which can be dried and used as food
ramekin	a small baking dish
rennet	an animal or vegetable substance that contains enzymes to curdle milk in cheese-making
salmonella	a harmful type of bacteria that can cause illness
saturated fat	a type of fat that is harmful to the body because it builds up in the arteries and causes heart disease
skimmed	thinned by removing cream from the surface
sterilised	treated to kill bacteria
tenderise	to make meat tender, or easy to chew, by breaking down its tough fibres
vats	large tanks
vitamin	a special substance found in food, which the body needs in tiny amounts to stay healthy
whey	the watery part of milk

Food safety

Each year there are about 70,000 food poisoning cases reported in the UK alone. Sticking to some simple rules can help you to avoid this and other kitchen dangers.

1. Clean all your work surfaces before you start cooking.

2. If you have long hair, tie it back away from your face.

3. To avoid a serious injury, always wear shoes in the kitchen.

4. Wash your hands well with soap and warm water before you start to cook. Wash them after handling any raw meat, poultry or fish.

5. Read through the recipe you are cooking before you start. Check that you have all the equipment and ingredients that you will need.

6. Check the sell-by dates on all food.

7. Wash all fruit and vegetables under cold running water.

8. When preparing food, keep it out of the refrigerator for the shortest time possible. Generally, you should not leave food out of the fridge for more than two hours.

9. Use a different chopping board and knife to prepare meat, chicken and fish from the one you use for preparing fruit and vegetables.

10. Never serve undercooked food, ensure that any meat, fish and chicken is cooked all the way through.

11. Replace used tea towels regularly with clean, dry ones to avoid the spreading of bacteria.

KNOW YOUR FOOD

Useful information
These abbreviations have been used:

ml – millilitre **g** – gram
cm – centimetre **mm** – millimetre

1 teaspoon = 5 millilitres
1 tablespoon = 15 millilitres

All eggs are medium unless stated.

Cooking temperatures:
To work out where the cooker dial needs to be for high, medium and low heat, count the marks on the dial and divide them by three. The top few are high, the bottom few are low and the in-between ones are medium.

Useful techniques

Kneading
Place the dough on a lightly floured surface. Press down on the dough with the palm of your hand, then fold the dough over itself and press down again. Continue to do this until the dough is soft and elastic.

Double cooking
By placing a bowl over a saucepan of boiling water, cream and more delicate ingredients cook slowly enough to ensure that they do not burn.

Making a well
To make a well in a mixture of dry ingredients, use a spoon to push the ingredients away from the centre of the bowl. You should end up with the ingredients on the outer edges of the bowl, and a gap or 'well' in the middle.

Creaming
When butter is at room temperature, put it with the required sugar into a bowl. Mix them together until they become a pale yellow, creamy colour.

Rubbing in
Use your fingertips to 'squash' the butter into the flour – the flour will look lumpy. Continue to rub in the butter until the flour resembles breadcrumbs.

Index

Useful websites

For information on ingredients and cookery techniques, log on to:

http://thefoody.com/basic/index.html or
http://www.bbc.co.uk/food/glossary/

For step-by-step video guides to cookery techniques, log on to:

http://www.waitrose.com/food/cookingandrecipes/cookinglibraries/howtovideos.aspx

For recipes for every occasion as well as tips for planning menus, log on to

http://www.bbc.co.uk/food/recipes/

FOOD & HOW TO COOK IT!

Contents of titles in series:

WAYLAND